Nocturne in Chrome & Sunset Yellow

Selected as one of the country's Next Generation poets, shortlisted for the 2004 Sunday Times Young Writer of the Year and named by the *TLS* as one of the best young writers in the country, Tobias Hill is one of the leading British writers of his generation. His award-winning collections of poetry are *Year of the Dog*, *Midnight in the City of Clocks*, and *Zoo*. His fiction has been published to acclaim in many countries. A.S. Byatt has observed that "There is no other voice today quite like this."

Also by Tobias Hill

POETRY

Year of the Dog (National Poetry Foundation, 1995)
Midnight in the City of Clocks (OUP, 1996; Carcanet, 2004)
Zoo (OUP, 1998)

SHORT STORIES

Skin (Faber, 1997)

NOVELS

Underground (Faber, 1999)
The Love of Stones (Faber, 2001)
The Cryptographer (Faber, 2003)

Nocturne in Chrome & Sunset Yellow

Tobias Hill

SALT

CAMBRIDGE

PUBLISHED BY SALT PUBLISHING

PO Box 937, Great Wilbraham, Cambridge PDO CB1 5JX United Kingdom

© Tobias Hill, 2006

The right of Tobias Hill to be identified as the
author of this work has been asserted by him in accordance
with Section 77 of the Copyright, Designs and Patents Act 1988.

First published 2006

Printed and bound in the United Kingdom by Lightning Source

Typeset in Swift 9.5 / 13

ISBN-13 978 1 84771 262 5 paperback
ISBN-10 1 84771 262 1 paperback

SP

1 3 5 7 9 8 6 4 2

to HD

Contents

Acknowledgments

Thanks are due to the editors of the following publications where some of these poems first appeared. 'The Orator' and 'Five Ways of Looking at my Grandfather (I)' were published online by *The Guardian*. 'The Gifts' was published in *London Magazine*. 'Repossession', 'Horse Chestnuts' and the sequence 'A Year in London' were published in *PN Review*. 'The Nightworkers' was published in *Poetry Review*. 'From the Diaries of Henry Morgan, Summer 1653' was published in *The Rialto*. 'Gravity' was published in the *Times Literary Supplement*.

'A Bowl of Green Fruit' was commissioned for the first wedding anniversary of Guini and Phil Webster. 'The Lighthouse Keeper's Cat' was commissioned by the Royal Mail to accompany their New Millennium stamps entitled *Life on Earth*. Both stamps and poem were issued in April 2000.

'Yellow' was anthologised in *Last Words*, edited by Don Paterson and Jo Shapcott (Picador, 1999).

To paint the sea really well, you need to look at it every hour of every day in the same place so that you can understand its ways in that particular spot.

CLAUDE MONET.

Cities give us collision.

R.W. EMERSON.

From the Diaries of Henry Morgan, Summer 1653

And so on May Day's eve I came to London,
with John Twentyman still riding beside me,
still chastising London even as we entered her,
her great steeples rising northwards and everywhere
bells, like those of towns in certain stories,
arisen from the sea on just such nights as these.

A dour and good man John Twentyman seemed,
and prudish in all he said, remarking
that the country life is much to be preferred,
there being Works of God there, and herein
nothing that has not been touched
into its present form by the hands of men;
but I have heard poor word of him since then,
and think the less of him for his hypocrisies.

As to myself, I have since had
much joy of London. My nights have been
as nights spent in the company of lovers.
I have played merry and yet have made
much good of myself. I am eighteen,
and have chattels and lace enough
by which a stranger might judge me a fine man.
I have a brace of snaphaunce from Tourner's,
and a sword all out of Damascene.

I do not think I will go home again.
God willing, I will make my home
hie to me as it were a good mare
coming up to the Bishop's Gate
and shaking her white head
at all the bells and carillons of London.

Repossession

The first we heard of it was the silence.
There was a morning with seagulls in it.
The air was grey, and held the smell of salt,
and when the rain began at last, at noon,

a black van pulled in by the off-license,
so silently you had to look, and out
got the bailiffs . . . unassuming men, not
well-built as you might expect, or even

wide in the shoulders. They went to the house
with the flying buttresses where the road
gives out at the end onto railway land,
and took the door right off its hinges, one

talking down to the other in a voice
so gentle it might never have been used
to speak of violence. Which is what they did,
the smaller of them each time carrying

the chattels out, while the tall one appraised
the estimated value of the bed,
the clothes-wringer, the clothes, even some seeds
the people there had meant to plant that Spring.

They frogmarched metal shutters from the van
and bolted down the door and the windows.
Then they were done, and the van was pulling
away into the rain, which smelled of tides,

the rime blown thirty miles from Southend,
and the couple who lived in that last house
came home, the woman first, trying her hand
at kicking down doors, the man returning

later, one or the other coming round
for the loan of a crowbar. Her hands bled
before they left. We saw them again once,
by chance, the two of them sat next to us

in traffic East of Clapton. None of us
had the time to wave, and neither of them
really seemed to see us there, their faces
turning just then to look at something else.

An accident, perhaps. This isn't what
I meant to talk to you about.
The thing is this.

After the repossession men had gone
the place went up for auction, but no one
offered a price. The bank was stuck with it.
And years went by, in which the house became

homeless. The garden sank down in a tide
of lost property. Shopping trolleys stacked
with shopping bags and shopping magazines
and bottles full of groundwater and mould

suspended like marvels of medicine
and earth accumulated by the rain.
The bushes garlanded with two-for-one
takeaway menus, tin cans, foam cups, string,

the straight-backed chair where foxes sat enthroned,
the mattress where an old man slept all Spring,
the kitchen sink full of the earthenware
of mushrooms and cracked blocks of Thermalite
dumped there, as if someone once meant to build
on those foundations of abandonment.

All this was years ago. And now you're here,
the two of you scything the bittersweet,
hopeful and very young, pulling up weeds,
weeding discarded shirts and shoes and skirts,

cutting the brambles off above the roots
so that you'll see them back before too long,
but here you are all the same, both of you
young enough not to give up for the want

of trying. And you've come at the right time,
in Spring. Already the garden you've cleared
is taking in the air, the taste of salt
the wind brings thirty miles from the sea.

Soon crocuses will break up to the light,
yellow as eggs cracked clean into a glass,
and flowers that you never knew were there
or never knew were real will appear

out of the yard the bank once tried to own,
and finding themselves nothing else to wear,
will put on buds that open to the air
like mouths containing promises, like hands

containing gifts, like small fists opening
in gestures that say *Here*, and which say *Here*.

To a Boy on the Underground

The laptop cauls your face with light,
unflattering and glutinous.
The iPod plugs your ears with ambient noise.
If you would only disconnect

you'd see the Underground's dark tract
unearthed. The tube train coiling out
into sharp shadows, sunlight cutting in
between ramrod Victorian blocks,

and the sous-chef or waiter who basks
in the sun in a restaurant backyard,
and the underwriters, auditors or clerks
who lean out of high windows like the girls

in folklore, one dangling a cigarette,
one seeming to be savouring the smells
of pizza ovens, Peking duck and piss,
the air half-edible and wholly foul,

and here and there green hanging gardens,
sunken gardens, roof gardens,
yards like cesspits, and everywhere carnivals
of people, the crowds embracing their collision.

Only disconnect, and all this will be yours, my son.

A Year in London

(A Free Advertisement for Kabul John's Café, Kilburn Market)

You're late, you're late, you're late the blackbird says,
and true enough the starlings are settling,
jostling and scuffling the snow from the trees,
imitating console games and children's cries
and mobile phones and traffic lights and what might be
the trajectory of an unidentified flying object,

and night is closing in so fast,
the day so ahead of itself
that those in search of some last purchase
go lolloping through the snow,
clopping and crumping through the fresh white fall
into the fish-grey slush between the market pitches,

and the stalls are all packing up for the night,
the man at Max Classic Trade Price Shoes
and the woman at Wanshika's Quality Underwear
who might be Wanshika in the flesh
putting away their luxury goods,
leaving nothing behind that isn't
firmly nailed to the pavement.

The lights under the covered walks
are switched off one by one, until
only Kabul John's Café is lit,
its neon spanning out into the street,

the smell of All Day English Breakfast Specials
expanding in the January air
as thick as lard. So warm and nourishing
that passersby with nowhere left to go
stop in their tracks, breathe its emollient,

open the foggy sheet glass door,
stamp the mire from their boots,
sigh out the cold, and bow, and enter in.

FEBRUARY

Hungover, and forgetting to bring water,
I lean by the Leg of Mutton Pond
and watch the dogs that come to drink.

The tallest go in like horses,
slake their thirsts, and stagger out
skeletonized, glabrous, and still proud.

They mean no harm to anyone,
and warm the earth by virtue of their shit.
Under the oaks by West Heath Road
the soil is fertile and sweet
and loathsome as mechanically recovered meat.

Nothing will express its gratitude
today, but in the next week or the next,
snowdrops will thaw into the nourishment.

The corms of winter aconites
will go off like long-buried ordnance,
the English lawns will lock their roots
into trace elements of blood and bone,
the little shreds of life that are the birds
will expurgate the soil in their hunger,

and the first crocus that grows there
will unfurl its vermilion innards,
unsheathe its tenuous head,
and finding goodness in the world—
and much not good, but to its liking—
will satisfy its own thirst on the rich, bright air.

MARCH

Up at 4 a.m. to piss,
you are surprised by yesterday's rain
still tapping at the skylight to be let in.

Such patience. No friend of ours
invited for an evening
would wait so long for either of us.

You are still skinned with sleep as warm as milk,
so that you say to the rain, *I'm not dressed yet,*

and hear the wind in the chimney-breast
answer, *I own this ground and will again,*
in one gust, and in the next,
Nothing is for nothing.

You see the kitchen table has been laid
with a clean slate of moonlight,
and the bills we've not yet paid
for the winter months of North Sea gas
have been arranged like place settings.

At night, this house is not ours to own,
and something else receives its visitors.
A helicopter overhead goes
ploughing through the force which drives the rain,
the chopper moving closer, house to house
along the empty course of Watling Street
as if it too has been invited.

And the rain at the threshold still says nothing,
but taps and taps to be let in,
and the wind lodged in the chimney shrieks,
I own this acreage,
and will again. Nothing is for nothing.

APRIL

The first chess players have returned,
seven old men in shy grey tweeds
outside L'Algeroise Café,
their hands among the pawns, hungry as birds
eating a field bare of seed in Spring.

One is resolving problems from *The Times*,
one sips a tulip-glass of Turkish tea,
one licks his lips and risks his queen to check,
one chain-smokes with the sun warm on his back.

One talks incessantly, remembering games
in Budapest and Oran and Marseilles.
One eats small almond pastries from L'Algeroise,
his sweet fingers congealing to the pieces.
The last sits with a child on his knee
and plays with her as if she is a game
he has no talent for, but means to learn.

Cars head past like a river tide in Spring.
The grocer's boy from the Food & Wine
spills pears and avocados in the gutter
and goes down on his knees to rescue them.
Old women with high colour in their cheeks
buy leavened bread and withered aubergines.
The hoarding on the Bon Pain Bakery
changes from Ford to Marlboro to Lynx
to Chanel Number 5 and back again,

and by L'Algeroise, only the child
looks up from the rooks and sees that Spring
is drawing in beside her like a train,
all belch and brass and noise; that Spring
is just arriving all around her,

the look on her face going up and away,
over the old men at their games,
over the boy who is rescuing pears,
over the hoardings and aubergines,
up like a kite she goes into the Spring.

MAY

The street outside jointed with leery boys
and girls dressed up as sweethearts for the night
and buntings of blood draped in the gutters
where half the bouncers weigh into a fight,

or worse, weigh up the odds and make themselves
scarce as needs be when one needs must to piss.
Like two fat ladies from the bingo hall
next door, they shake their heads at all the mess:

like sumo wrestlers bored of slender wives
they look hungry for more, all petulance
and disappointment with the muck and maul
spilling across the street, as if they'd hoped

for better things tonight. For more than this,
the girls down on their knees, missing their shoes
in all the fuss. And still there are the queues
of punters loving it, waiting their turns

to push inside, into the sallow gloom
where the ticket woman and the cloakroom man
wait for their offerings of coats and coins
before they'll let a single soul pass through

into the wash of glitterball-spun light,
onto the dance floor, where the air is warm
and everyone is diamonded with stars,
where anyone can star in their own film,
a musical where star-crossed lovers meet
and dance, and slow-dance underneath the stars
until the stars themselves blush and wink out.

And though sequels are never half as good,
they're all the night's dancers will think about
as they walk out into the May-damp streets
alone or arm-in-arm, wrapped in their coats

or lacking even those. And Cricklewood
colder and darker than it was before,
the takeaways full of forlorn lovers
all much the worse themselves for wear and drink,

waving at taxis that slip past the lights
to Hampstead, where clients tip ten percent,
and not their guts, and don't try and get out
as soon as they see somewhere else they like,

and now there is no going back.
Ashtons is gone. The hall has been knocked down,
the land sold on. Pigeons sit
in rows along the hoardings, like
those boys who never brought themselves to dance
but stood all night and necked their beers:

Ashtons has closed for good,
and almost any night will find me glad,
loving the quiet as I work,
as I work now, or make us food, or wait
for my own love to come home through the dark,

and only once, walking home
from some night better never spent,
it seemed to me that the Broadway missed
something. A quality of brightness,
as if the lights had gone out all at once
across the neighbourhood,

and I thought of this and that.
Mostly the girls, who were pretty sometimes,
and always seemed to be looking for things
they'd either not yet found, or left behind
somewhere else. Their best friends and best earrings,

their drinks and shoes and coats and darling boys,
and dreams and last dances and happy endings.

JUNE

But Cricklewood is mine. I discovered it. No one will go there again. It is like the sunken town in the fairy story that rose just every May Day eve and lived for an hour and only one man saw it.

T.S.ELIOT, 1911.

Someone in that house must be in love
with scented geraniums:
there are so many of them,
all bunched and grubby and alive
out in the whitewashed yard.

I thought it was the younger
of the old tight-lipped black-eyed women
both of whom now and then
slouches out onto the steps,
squats down by the slipshod pots,
and leans up to the baskets
on tiptoes in green-furred slippers
with a long-necked green watering-can.

But neither of them ever seems
to take much pleasure in the task,
and after all, it could be the men
who find loveliness in that garden,

one of the Serbs or the Bosnian,
or the Corfiot who always looks
down at heel but in good spirits,
or the shy Somali in the eastern-facing room
who lives his days out in night-shifts,
any of those who come to live
here, of all places.

After all, why not them?
They are all single men, and prone to love.
On warmer evenings they come outside
to sit in the boarding house yard
and play at backgammon, or read
second-hand paperbacks
in their several alphabets.

Once, with a fence needing repair
we went there looking for labour.
The windowsills were stacked
with working mens' shoes
and cartons of milk.
The hallway was unlit and sour
with the odour of linoleum,

and the man who took the work
came early the next day,
refused the food we offered,
ate his own, and worked
until the light was gone outside,

carpenting the lengths of wood
with skill and patience and no word
of English but one for a greeting
and one more for thanks in the evening.

Afterwards we recognised him,
one man in several, walking home
along the dark blocks of the high road,
past the derelicts sat propped
in the doorways of derelicts,

none of them with a lift in their step,
each of them trudging home,
but somehow trudging home,
back to their accommodations,
the one room, the timed strip
of light above the washbasin:

back through the broken concrete
of the yard, the flowers thriving there
leaving a scent on each man's skin,
something for them to remember,

something to bring them back in years to come
here, to Cricklewood,
as if this was a time and place they ever loved.

JULY
(At the Wing Yip Chinese Supermarket)

The old fishmonger with the cropped grey hair
leaves to her young apprentices the tasks
she has no appetite left for,
and no longer takes pleasure from.

Her eyes slide over heaps of grey croaker
and customers she doesn't know by name,
though no one lifts the lobsters from their tanks
or fillets dog-shark except her:

to her go all the finer works.
She guts the yellowtail and gilthead bream,
the scales adhering to her braced forearm
until it seems transmogrified,

her skin shining, sequinned, and slicked with blood.
She beheads char, cuts through the spines
of congers, rinses viscera and bones
from her raw red knuckled fingers,

and goes out to the locked ice-room,
coming back in with sabrefish
unsheathed over her shoulderblades,
the cold escaping in a wash

of fog around her boots and jeans.
She looks in the eyes of the wealthy men
who buy such things, and nods, and says,

Yes, fresh.
The eyes of the great greyhoundish heads
laid meekly in her scaled hands
as cold and bright as jewels, or pommel stones.

AUGUST

when pigeons like *dei ex machina*
descend improbably out of the air

wobble like airships skimming through the tops
of trees which sink under their tea-pink weights

until each grandee bungee-jumps or bellyflops
downwards in great soap-operatic terrifying swoops

into the sweet dark shining feather-bedness of the fruits

SEPTEMBER

And sometimes months go by when London
leaves me cold, hating the starlessness
of its illuminated midnights
and the muck of noise on the Edgware Road
where a glut of goods is bought and sold
24-7. I lose my appetites,
wanting for nothing for so long
that I dream of nothing worth wanting,
not the pearskin lacquer furniture
stacked on the pavements, or the duckbone jade
the old men wear to fortify their hearts,
or the bagels trawled from boiling vats,
the lobsters knuckled down in blue-lit tanks,
or the girl in the summer dress who eats
priceless white peaches with the juice
running down her wrists like pale sinews,
or the basements impregnated with the smells
of tamarinds and naan and cooking wine,
or the people in the road outside
who seem to move in the way that starlings
hinge themselves together in the sky.

Then something will happen to make me remember
what it is I love here,
what I am wanting for. It will be some grey September.
I will look outside.

In the garden
the goldfish are nuzzling
at heaps of soft late summer rain.

If I could have only one thing,
it would be some moment like this,
when one small fact puts all the facts right,

when the rain clears the London air
and my thoughts lie suddenly clean
and bright in the strength of their own wellspring.

OCTOBER

October, and you buy pomegranates,
the Sabian grocer on Shoot Up Hill
putting one extra in the bag for you
because he insists it matches your hair,

which I had always thought was only brown,
chestnut at most, like the nuggets of seeds
the trees in Gladstone Park are letting fall,
as if I'd never looked at you at all.

I will never have seen enough of you.

NOVEMBER

London — there's a rhythm to the name,
its ending an echo of its beginning,
as if *London* were the name for somewhere
full to the brim with its own echoes.

I think of the sound of ordnance
each November, the guns echoing
through the fog and the minute's silence
in remembrance of themselves,

and the bomb's echo that shook the air
miles north of the Natwest Tower
the night my father came cycling home,
shepherding the bike into the hall
before he said he wasn't feeling well,
his heart foundering in our hands,

and the sound of fireworks, that night
we stopped on the stairs in Bell Wharf Lane
to watch them fall across the river,

the thunderous openings like hands, or
arms thrown wide in embraces,
each one falling short of our places
on the black steps of the wharfside stairs.

Those rockets coming down in glorious gold
into the river. Who were they for?
How would we ever know? The echoes
filling up the streets around us
with a sound like *London*, a sound like *Lon*

Don. And all that brilliance was ours
in our dreams that night, even
if none of it was ever meant for us.

December

What frost there was is nearly gone by the time I'm up to look for it. I
take a book I'm meant to read and go up the hill to Gladstone Park. The
Pleasure Grounds are still unlocked. The air is pricked with awns of ice
that settle in my two-week beard. A man on the bench by the ginkgo tree
hunkers down against the cold. He cups his cigarettes against the frost,
smokes each one to the end and drops the ends between his feet. He tips
the ash from a fifth before he crushes it out under his foot. He waits for
the last to cool before he picks them up, one by one, and puts them back
in the golden packet. He takes it with him when he goes.

I walk home past the pumping station. One day they'll sell it off for flats.
Inside its nave, the reservoir casts slatted ripples up the walls. They say
ice is lighter than water. As a child I thought it hung above the ponds on
the Heath like the vaults of churches. At the Irish butcher's I buy what I
can for the change in my pocket. Indoors, I cut the meat, slide it along the
knife and board, into the pot of leftovers, letting it warm over the flame.
Outside the snow begins. The light on the phone has lit itself. I leave it
and take off my coat. I go upstairs in the dark, holding onto my thoughts.
Balancing them, one ripple against the other, as if I were carrying water.

TV Dinner

You at the counter, cutting onions into moons,
one hand aloft to heel away the tears,

me watching ants on the television,
two of them, drinking a bridal cup
of rain, holding the drop between them,
the bright waterskin unbroken.

The clock by the window striking nine,
the pendulum drowsing,
the ants drinking from their upheld moon,

and you coming to stand beside me,
your hand coming to rest on me,
your eyes on the television,
and your face all wet and salt from weeping.

Synthesis

Cutting into colour,
wormcasts and turds of cadmium,

chiselling the new violet,
squibs and swabs of cobalt blue,

drilling one iota of lead white
into an ammonite of best vermilion,

Matisse feels as if he is
a sculptor carving into stone.

Somewhere, he once came across
a line of Pliny, old and sour,
bristling at younger pleasures,

Now India contributes the ooze of her rivers
and the blood of dragons and of elephants—
his picked bone being Rome's painters
dipping their wicks in shameless eastern taints.

It is summer, and every year
he still comes back to Paris
having wintered in Nice,
though there's no peace here for anyone.
It is a congeries of passersby
and motorcars and early callers,

the synthesis of light and noise
unnatural as the latest pigments
sold for a packet at Sennelier's,
the brightest new ultramarine,
or the brown mummy, which is composed
of no embalmed flesh, the Egyptians
having brought that trade to an end.

But here he is again,
back in the city in high summer,
chipping germs of pigment from the palette,

and still finding
how much he loves
the way that as dawn breaks
the sounds of the street below
fade up and penetrate into this room,

just as the arsenic in the violet
has penetrated his fingers,
turning their whorled impressions
into ten works of vivid synthesis.

Gravity

How can there have been a time when this
still lay undiscovered: light falling
through the trees, and the first leaves falling
all at once into the cold evening,
leaves through light in endless gravity?

By the church where I sang as a boy
and dreamed I'd be a scientist
I break my walk, and sit quite still.

How still must I sit to hear the dead?
Through the obduracy of the yews
the wind shuffles and stills and runs on

into the fallen leaves by the locked church door,
with the sibilance of the Lord's Prayer.

Forgive us our trespasses.
Dusk falls into the streets.

The owl quarters its territories.
Still I am not still enough.

The Gifts

Fishing the warm newspaper off his chips,
Now, where have I seen that before? he said,
and smoothed it out in the street with the wind
worrying at the parcels in our hands.

And there was nothing printed there but words.
His words, worked at, meant as the best of him,
marked up with sauce and vinegar, and scraps
and haddock shovelled in over his name.

I thought his pride was hurt, and understood
nothing then of the writer's pride he found
in coming on his words like that. Strangers
queuing for them in the shop's salt brightness,

and, block by block, nursing them through the streets
like long-awaited news. Like heartfelt gifts.

The Nightworkers

Long after midnight
the railwaymen
work in pairs along the line
surreptitiously, at first,

the track stones
under their boots
trod like ice
into ruts.

The clocks stop for them.
Nothing comes
while they mend their ways.
Nothing goes. The night trains

rest in their stables.
The mainline lies
bright as cobweb

and the voice of the first man to speak
becomes a grand thing in the darkness
and the workers who follow
lope like so many bogeymen
through the lights of the gantry towers.

≈

We lie awake for hours.
We rise like sleepers
hauled from beds of stone.
We cannot close our ears to the North
the railwaymen bring in their laughter.

Only towards morning will a word
turn them, one by one
homewards, calling names
and names and goodbyes as they go,

and though we'll be released to sleep
we'll lie awake in those small hours
until we're sure we've heard the last
there is to hear. We'll hang on their words,

listening for the lightness in them,
the lift in their voices at first light,
the eagerness they have in going home,
and even for the way they seem
to wake from sleep or dreams themselves,

as if they've slept their lives away, and now
find themselves boys again, waking in winter
to yell their names clear across miles of snow.

The Orator

The people of Amathus, in revenge for his having laid siege to their town,
severed the head from the dead body of Onesilus and hung it up above their
gates. In time it became hollow, and was occupied by a swarm of bees, who
filled it with honeycomb.'

HERODOTUS, 'THE HISTORIES'

Monday finds him early at his station,
squatting on his haunches on the corner
outside Barclays Bank, eating hand-me-downs
from McDonald's, then unfolding long shanks,
pocketed hands, and a skull losing hair
as if someone in love has stroked him there
more often than the flesh of him can bear,

and so comes to a standstill, his back flat
to the thronged house of the moneylenders,
the first words already poised on his lips,
the rest of them gathering up inside,
until he lifts his bandaged megaphone
and opens up his teeth to let them out.

THOSE WHO COME TO FIND THE LORD
—Napthalis says through a plague of static—
THOSE WHO WAIT TO LOOK FOR HIM
ONLY AT THE ELEVENTH HOUR
WILL DIE AT TEN THIRTY, Napthalis says,

but the English rain has again begun
its interrupted centuries of fall
and no one stops to listen, though some
look back at him with surreptitious spite,

the man with the golden bee in his bonnet,
the figure in the knitted cap and parka
with God lodged like a dove in his mind,
and a curse on the house of each commuter:
sharp as splinters lodged in careless hands
are his offerings, his diatribes.

Not even a smile on a swan-black girl
assuages him. But the days are long,
and evenings find him murmuring
the spirituals that his aunts taught him,
the old women with ermine eyes,
tough as yardfowl, their mingled voices
sour-sweet as the juice of June plum,

and faint, so that they come to him now
only as visitations in his dreams;
Dara, with the dozen rings,
Maud, who sometimes read to him

when he was a boy in a town called Rest
in a house on the river on the green island
he hasn't seen in forty-seven years
and won't see again now before Heaven.

DO NOT HURRY INTO ETERNITY
he says with rationed fire and brimstone
to the overstanding gentleman
who stops to give him a toll of change
but should know better than to go

yarding through the rain like a madman,
sneezing all the way like a dog barking—
all teeth—to reach Iceland by closing time,

the newspaperman across the road
a balancing muezzin, when Napthalis
starts to hum again,
Isaiah a sweet venom on his tongue,
while the rain from the north stings his face,

and the sky is leaded with more to come,
or with the dark of the world that waits
to fall, Napthalis thinks, though he knows

that in Cricklewood on a Monday night
nothing is fit to bear the weight
of being anything more than it seems,

and just as Napthalis is just Napthalis,
so the darkness that surrounds him
is nothing more or less than darkness.

Amphibians

No cats out in this weather,
only the dog with its hair slicked flat
in the yard beside the timber depot,
and the fish in the blue garden urn
mouthing at the water's surface,

as if, when their gold lips break through its tension,
they'll swim out from their deep enamelled cistern
and up and up into the deep blue downpour.

The Lighthouse Keeper's Cat

In 1895 a new species of wren was discovered on St Stephen's Island off
New Zealand. The Stephen's Island Wren was only ever identified from dead
specimens, the last having been killed by the lighthouse keeper's cat.

All day it lies as if extinct,
coiled like an ammonite
at the foot of the spiral stairs,
or basks in the primacy of sunlight.

Only at night will it bring him gifts.
The lighthouse keeper wakes
to the watchworks of ghost crabs
left for dead, and to wrens so slight

that more than once he misses them,
and twice takes them for living things,
the fishbone teeth of the tom
having held them so carefully.

Before he came to the island
the keeper dreamed of the loneliness,
the rocks and the flotsam of the wrecks,
and found all this, but also found

the bright peoplings of birds,
the balance of hawk and gull
over green inland hills, swifts wintering,
and hummingbirds, greener than green.

He climbed the damp helix of stairs
and found the lamps on their axis
grown solid with a weld of rust,
fossilised in the wet salt air,

and nineteen days in the mending,
with only the eyes of the cat
moving around the rounded room,
the animal turning and turning about

like a warning of something happening
or yet to happen. Those first weeks
he slept not knowing yet what he had done,
not knowing that a part of him

left his side each night and went
out into the green and greener hills,
uncoiling under the lamp of the moon
to bring him back his small, delicate gifts.

Five Ways of Looking at my Grandfather

I

Here is Basil Philip's microscope,
human as the things humans possess
too deeply, loving too much
those possessions that come to possess them.

How well he cared for these six lenses,
each spare eye snug in its metal case,
each case nested in its velvet socket
like a shotgun shell cast out of brass.

The lidded cylinders have kept their shine,
the fragile concavities of glass
their strength. The measure of each gaze
is etched under the maker's sign,

and on the slides, with their salmon-fine
leaves of spinal nerve and miner's lung,
Doctor Basil Philip Hill has signed

his handiwork (his writing so small
that he might have been measuring out
valuable medicine, and not ink,

drop by blue Indian drop),
so that something of Basil Philip
survives him in his instrument,

even though nothing of him remains
on these cold surfaces; not so much
as a single fingerprint.

II

Here he is, his face pressed to the glass,
watching the blackbirds guzzling his redcurrants,

fingers leaving puzzled labyrinths
on the pantry window where he leans,

eyes (what colour were they? I recall
blue, but none of us are blue-eyed boys—)

blue eyes on the blackbirds, like a cat's,
the garden bright and still as tapestry

except for the birds, burgling the swags
of all the sweetness that he cares for,

so that he mutters at their flit and flicker,
and chews on his moustache, as if it could

nourish him, with such sweet nourishment
as birds might find on a cold morning,

and without knowing it, he grinds his teeth,
as if he means to drop the birds stone-dead,

as if he held those sweet throats in his mouth.

III

After the death of his middle son,
Basil Philip brooked no carelessness
and let the past into the future
as sparingly as he would measure
air and ether for the surgeon.

The dead were not to be seen or heard
in the house with the room where the boy had died,
but the room itself was full of nothing,
like a vacuum in a dome of glass,
and the air in that house always seemed
as botched and harmful as an overdose.

When was it that he gave up hope
of wedded love? Or was that her?
She grieved with less care for her happiness,
and many years before she died,
gave up also the ghosts of memories.

So one forgot, and one refused
to dwell on things better forgotten,
and neither chose to speak of it again.

And if they went on loving, then their love
was never seen or heard itself, as if
it wasn't something which they wished to prove
to anyone, and least of all themselves,

and if they did not, then the *not* was pushed
into a corner, like old medicine,
or hidden in the shadows of the house
like a child playing at hide-and-seek,

a boy crouched in the dusty attic dark,
listening to someone count a hundred
and wishing only never to be found.

IV

Each night, the headlights of his car
turn in late from the Royal Berkshire,
all the things that remain unsaid
there in the hall in the darkness with him,

and late at table, flushed, he asks for
carrots, mustard, sauce-boat, cruet
through the media of those who live,

comments on the cauliflower,
observations on the weather,
passed through one son or the other

as if they are concavities of glass
through which a man might know his wife
without having to catch her eyes.

He doesn't glance up when she drops her knife
but works his soup, head down, as if he eats
guesthouse food at a table by himself,

and so they all four eat as if alone.
Or as if, somewhere in the room, a fifth
stands like a man outside a restaurant,
drawn by the light, the foggy glass, the smell of meat,
wanting for company, or nourishment, or rest.

V

My favourite memory of him:
old and not much belittled
by the wrong-ended focus of the years,

moving a pumpkin from place to place
in the best room of a smaller house.

The fridge is full of chocolate,
great bars and cakes of it, and nothing else.
He has no one but himself to please.

He carries the fluted, green-gold weight
of the first pumpkin of the year
from the piano to the mantlepiece
to keep it in the ripening light,

as carefully as if, with his care,
all will be well in the end. As if,
with care, nothing will come to dispel

the light that settles on the windowsill
and gathers like a harvest in that room.

The Woman Who Likes Standing Under Trees in the Rain

The woman who likes standing under trees in the rain.
The woman who liked whistling like a man.
The woman who stayed a night and laughed
in her sleep. The woman who stayed a night
and who I didn't see again

for seven years, then stood there smiling
as if we'd never spent a night apart.
The woman who only liked kissing
heavy smokers. The woman who dreamt
I threw her from a moving train.
The woman who said *do what you want with me*
and wept when I did.

The woman who loved the smell of blood
and petrol stations. The woman who loathed
the smell of fireworks. The woman who hated
carnations, and never much liked music.

On journeys, stuck in traffic,
or leant to catch the small talk of a smoker,
or under the pyrotechnic flowers
of New Years' Eves and bonfires,

I catch myself thinking of them,
recalling what they did to me and me to them,
and don't wish there were more of them
half so much as I once did,

and still, will sometimes stop and try to think
what it was I ever liked or loved
about a woman who never much liked music.

Nine in the Morning in the Station Bar

What does the man in the old brown suit
say to the Old Masters on the wall
so softly that no one else can hear?

And what do the Masters say to him
that makes him flinch and turn to the room
and crow, his voice abruptly rising,

'You'll all be here till the cows come home,
bastards,' by which he means *forever*,
since no cow in a fit state of mind
would be seen dead or alive in here—

The Shire Bar, St Pancras station—
in this or any other century
(although the pub menu does offer
balti with the wording, *tender meat*).

The jukebox plays *Relax, Don't Do It*,
the TV with the sound turned down
follows the Teletubbies homewards,

and worst of all, the barman nods,
and one of the drinkers makes a face
as if to say that about trains, at least,
the old man in the suit is never wrong.

The Teletubbies rediscover shadows.
Frankie goes on and on to Hollywood.
Nine in the morning in the station bar,
and nobody comes in, and nobody goes home.

Yellow

All night she keeps the car radio on,
driving from station to station. Bhangra,
long waves, police calls, *Walking on the Moon.*
In the morning her life is behind her

and light comes shearing through the Southern rain.
She stops to take pictures of a rainbow,
the span of it above the contraflow
so still, as if nothing has yet fallen,

not her out of her life nor this downpour
through all the empty places of the sky.
Daffodils wave their yellow heads at her
and suddenly she thinks of poetry:

beautiful things. The perfect words you say
only later, too late, driving away.

A Bowl of Green Fruit

I ask for love;
she brings me breakfast kisses.
I ask my love for love
and she gives me green fruit in winter.

A bowl of green fruit.
Nothing ripe or ready.
Only the hard hearts of apples,
the acid in their whiteness,
the riddles of green oranges.

I say, I asked for love.
Why did you give me
a bowl of green fruit? She says;

wait.
And so we do,
the taste of the kisses

sweetening in our mouths,
the hearts softening,
the riddles undoing themselves.

The Wave

In the small hours, the first snow
falls and disappears and falls and

holds to itself,
the ground beneath already sprung with growth.

You bed the blunt new hyacinths in straw
and cut the last hard bud
from the damask rose you planted
last winter by the kitchen door,

and stand there with it in your hand,
out in the dead and buried yard,
as if you are asking yourself
What should I do with this?

How small my writing has become.
All day news of the dead rolls in.

We have observed the silences,
and given. What more can we give?

The death toll mounts every morning.
It grows unspeakable. You wash and dress

by the television's Morse of light,
the volume muted on the silences
which go on here and there around the world
and which, laid end to end, would render us
speechless for life. You check your purse,

keys, travelcard, and look back as you leave
in case you've left the television on,

as if the light that washes our dark room
could still come flooding out. Who would you save
if it did? And look, the flats above the shops
are all awash with that submarine light

that the news brings, and those out on the street
walk fast, as if each of them would escape
something unthinkable. This knowingness.
Nobody knows what else to do with it
but bear it, and it isn't finished yet.

There is much more that we could know,
and nobody can tell where it will stop,
or if it ever will. This is the news.
What should I do with this? you say, and then
What should I do with this?

Horse Chestnuts

Ever since summer blew their candles out
they've nursed their loss, and now their plots are hatched.

They've mined the wind. The thud of their hulls
sounds louder than our own footfalls
as we set out to walk away a night
spent poorly, in vindictive argument.

Under the avenues, the air is fogged
with the rancour and sulphur of leaf-rot,
chill after the first hard night of winter.

What's the good of talking, when our talk
brings us to this? And so we say nothing,
walking in silence under the silence
of the chestnuts, our quarrel growing
cold in the morning's greater coldness;

so, bit by bit, the day belittles us,
and with us our mistakes. Our slights seem slight
under the limbs that overshadow us
where nothing cares for us, but nothing cares
how long it takes for us to make things right.

We walk until, by silent compromise,
our hands brush past each other, and then hold.

Hold fast, my love, because there is still good
in what we have, and we will find it out.
Because there is still good for us to give,
and one to the other we will give it.

Hold tight. There's good in us, as there is
inside the sharp, green hulls of the chestnuts,
which open as we tread them underfoot,

halving to reveal themselves, not cold,
or spent, but bright as bloody, beating hearts.

Summer Late Night Opening

My god is this whole bloody place
gone to the bloody dogs tonight?
says the man in second place
behind the woman with blue hair
at checkout number five, his face
slick as the sleach in the street outside
where the roadmenders have left the road unmade.

Here is a soul who by default
moves through his days slouched like a bear,
his musculature buried under
rolls and cauls of spoiled fat
until he rears upright in anger
—as he does now—his nylon shirt
stained through with sweat from crotch to shoulder.

What's wrong with everyone tonight?
he says, and, *Is this lady mad?*
he asks, but finds he gets no answer,
because to disagree might goad him further,
and to agree would be too rude,

since, yes, the blue woman seems mad,
something in her gone haywire,
 the balance of the air around her
full of the frizz and fizz and slide
of whatever thing it is that ails her.

She has now packed her shopping cart
so many times we've all lost count,
each time unpacking it again
to stare down at the things she's bought
in frank, innocent wonderment:
the eggs as smooth as eggs!
the Stagg Silverado Chicken-in-a-Can!

That's it! exclaims the ursine man,
and shambles out into the street
without the rice he meant for supper.

On the way home we see her again,
the vision of the blue woman,
standing by the green traffic lights,
gazing up with her mouth open
as if they are a visitation.

What is wrong with us tonight?
It is the first evening of June
and the crowds are out on the streets.
Everyone is coming down
like children out of school for summer.

Perhaps we are a little mad.
The air around us hums with it.
Perhaps we are all mad with hunger,
mad with everything that hunger
might conceivably be felt for.

Which is to say—mad for each other;
mad for these short nights of summer;
mad for the heat of the darkness
in which the moths above us
burn themselves up like comets
in the auras of the streetlights,
in the pleasures of their madness.

Nocturne

Full moon tonight
and the snow falling,
as if the moon could shine so bright
that it would melt the snow by morning.

Chiswick Eyot
to Whistler's Mooring,
Bell Wharf Stairs to the Embankment,
Dark House Steps to the Barrier Building—

How far you've walked,
though you've been walking
this way so long you can forget
what year it is or where you're going.

This is constant:
the river's passing,
the undertow of its descent,
though all around it has been changing

every minute,
the city nothing
if not forever inconstant.
Some days you can't escape the feeling

that all is spent,
that you are running
out like the Thames into the waste
of the scoured North Sea: that there's nothing

still to be learnt,
or no more learning
that you would want to have by heart,
having no want left for anything.

Eat Your Heart Out
says the lit hoarding
up on the bridge by Parliament,
the snowflakes dancing and skimmering

as they go out,
white sparks vanishing
into the river's firmament.
This is the vein and the heart of it,

the Thames at night,
the city sleeping
under the clock tower's movement,
the slow toll of Big Ben foundering

up in the white,
and all this carving,
the generals poised in granite,
the dragon-skulls and cannon-bones

of horses rendered into stones,
the sentinels of kings and queens,
the epigraphs of the ammonites.

Are we there yet?
Something is saying
just ahead, where the dearth of light
hides anything it might be doing.

Are we there yet?
like a kid whining
by the turning, in the blind spot
you didn't mean to find this evening

or any night.
You must be leaving.
Don't look back now. Pick up your feet,
and keep walking. *And keep on walking*

Printed in the United Kingdom
by Lightning Source UK Ltd.
117907UK00001B/115-213